The Cloud of Unknowing

In Light of the Unborn

Vajragoni

Dragonyana Press

ISBN: 979-8-218-21237-7

FOREWARD

This work originally appeared on our website,
UnbornMind.com. UnbornMind Zen is a
derivative of Ch'an Buddhism, with a special
emphasis upon the sacred text of the
Lankavatara Sutra. As Lankavatarians, our
foundation is based on the ancient mantra,
"What the Mind focuses on determines its
Reality"; in league with Cittamatra, or the
Mind Only school of Zen Buddhism. It is part
of an ongoing series of blog posts beginning
in 2011 revolving around Buddhist themes,
scriptures and associated spiritualities. We
offer a veritable storehouse of Noble Wisdom
encapsulating thousands of pages devoted to
the Buddhadharma—all of this bracketed by
the spirit of the Prajnaparamita. In reference
to this present work, a classic of Western
Spirituality, my own background as priest and
as an eremitical ascetic of the Lankavatarian
path places me squarely in both traditions
thus offering a unique vantage point
concerning Ascetical Contemplation. Many
times Contemplation is misunderstood and
rendered as a secondary spiritual tool
following meditation. However,

Contemplation, as utilized and experienced through the works of Mystical Giants like the author of The Cloud and John of the Cross, perhaps draws the spiritual adept intimately closer to the Unborn than any other modality. There are two primary forms of Contemplation. Active Contemplation utilizes many different types of experiential tools in encountering the Transcendent: reading, imagination, music, monastic liturgical settings, walking, attunement with nature, etc. Infused Contemplation, which is the core of this present work, means being stripped naked of all phenomena and what is left is the all-piercing awareness of the Absolute AS Absolute—undivided and devoid of all secondary characteristics. The primary factor to consider here is that of ascesis, or the deafening silence and solitude that are part and parcel of the spiritual discipline required in which to undertake such an audacious task. Infused Contemplation is a passive one, devoid as it is of all action thus opening itself to the movement of the primordial spirit. It's a self-emptying in order to be filled with the Absolute Fullness of the Unborn. Pure

Contemplatives, therefore, live a life of total solitude in the dark silence of the Great Void that is devoid of all defiling characteristics. This rendition of The Cloud of Unknowing is written in Light of the Unborn—meaning those associated spiritual principles found within UnbornMind Zen. The text is followed by a commentary. All in all, it's an eclectic work designed to dissolve the barriers of sectarianism that prevents one from directly experiencing a Contemplative spiritual path that is open to all, regardless of their religious orientations; such is the beauty of these Universal Truths whose Light shines upon all.

INTRODUCTION

Of all the texts of genuine Mysticism no other work has been translated as numerous times than the Anonymous, The Cloud of Unknowing. It was written by a 14th century Western Mystic and even unto this day his true identity is unknown. The renowned Anglican Mystic, Evelyn Underhill, writes, "The mystic who seeks the divine Cloud of Unknowing is to be surrendered to the direction of his deeper mind, his transcendental consciousness: that "spark of the soul" which is in touch with eternal realities." The author utilizes the image of two clouds: the cloud of unknowing above us and the cloud of forgetting beneath us. The cloud of unknowing represents the realization that God is beyond our ability to perceive through our senses, emotions, imagination, or intellect. Again, from Underhill, "The conception of reality which underlies this profound and beautiful passage, has much in common with that found in the work of many other mystics; since it is ultimately derived from the great Neoplatonic philosophy of the contemplative life." With this foremost in mind the present version, The Cloud of Unknowing in Light of the Unborn, is written in such a literary vein.

Its predecessors at Unborn Mind Zen are *The Dhammapada in Light of the Unborn*, and The Bhagavad Gita (again, written in Light of the Unborn). Ours is a singular spiritual convention, dating back to the earliest adepts of the Lanka. My own background, in light of the present task, places me in both traditions—one as priest and as an eremitical ascetic of the Lankavatarian path. This is a valuable fact since there have been those who would discourage others from reading The Cloud since they are not of the Catholic Contemplative tradition. My background permits me the license to undertake this series since my spiritual experience is from both camps. That being said, this will be a most daring undertaking as The Cloud itself is a most extraordinary mystical text, perhaps even grander than the works of St. John of the Cross himself. Here in such fashion is the paradox of a contemplation that is at once Christocentric and imageless. Of course, our work will be Buddhocentric along with that imageless factor.

Preamble-Take Counsel

Great Homage to the Unborn Lord! Dear Sojourner, please attend well: Whoever you may be coming into possession of these spiritual truths, I strongly urge that before you read any further to comprehend that this undertaking entails a most serious responsibility. Never present these teachings to those of shallow or callous mindsets. Do your utmost to discern well beforehand whether they have a genuine interest in such pursuits or are just busybodies out to profane the Buddhadharma. Rather, be diligent and utmost aware that skillful sincerity is foremost present. They must be those who are open to honor and treasure such spiritual delights. Foremost, they must be adepts who are prepared to attend well the Spirit of Contemplation. If they are exclusively attached to methods of active meditation, then this is definitely no territory for them to investigate and wholeheartedly embrace as their own. On the other hand, if they are presently engaged in active spiritual methods but somehow sense in their mind and spirit the need for further and higher spiritual cultivation, then by all means encourage them to do so. But firstly charge them with the same caveat I have presented to you. I am especially referring to those who have tasted the fruit of mysterious inward luminosity and now yearn for full unionship in the Unborn. So then, my dear spiritual friend in the Unborn, continually examine and take prudent observance over your own spiritual cultivation. With all your beingness thank the Unborn Lord and ask that his Dharma Protectors keep careful watch over you and prevent any spiritual assaults of Mara the evil one from ever taking hold. May you come to win the full prize that awaits your resolute determination.

Commentary

Like the original intent from the author of The Cloud, our text begins with a qualified caveat: what's being presented is not for anyone with just idle curiosity. It is meant for those Noble Ones who will apply the effort and "will" necessary to respond in body, mind, and spirit to what transcendent treasures are being freely given unto them. Are you in earnest over your own spiritual cultivation? Then this text will provide the required spiritual tools to climb that Noble Mountain of Primordial Perfection. If not, then lay this aside for now and continue in your own measured pace of cultivation that is best for you.

1. The Four Stages

DISCOURSE ONE

Of the four degrees in Buddhist life
And how the adept for whom this treatise was written
Would advance in his spiritual vocation.

Dear Spiritual Friend in the Unborn, you need
to be aware what I have observed concerning
the formation of the Buddhist Path. There are
four degrees of Buddhist Living. *Common,*
Special, Singular, and Perfect. The first three may
be completed during this present life-cycle;
but the fourth, which begins here, continues
without end in the bliss of Nirvana. Firstly,
you are already aware of how you pursued the
Unborn path in common-fellowship with
your fellow sojourners, until such time that
the Transcendent Calling of the Unborn Spirit
instilled in your heart the realization that the
Absolute was calling you to something far
more profound. Therefore, in Infinite
Compassion, the Unborn Lord instilled that
Special yearning to be at One with Him
Alone. He was calling you to be his friend and
so come to live in a Special manner of living
that you were to become an adept among his
own Special adepts. In this fashion he drew
you infinitely closer to enjoy the inward

spiritual life more undividedly than when you lived among the common herd. And what is more? From the very beginning its design for you could not leave you uncompleted, and so you have been drawn-forth to the Singular Way, awakening that deep and solitary core of your very being. And there you shall now rest until the state of Perfection draws nigh.

Commentary

The four stages: *Common*, living the ordinary Buddhist life, meditating, reading, exchanging ideas with others on the path; *Special*, making the extra effort to go beyond mere study and comfort in meditation in order to advance towards a higher contemplative spiritual realization; *Singular*, beyond this point one comes into contact with a spirit of transcendence, issuing-forth the complete turn-about from one's former efforts and now being determined to seek deeper spiritual truths; *Perfect*, the adept now makes a complete break from society, seeking out eremitic solitude alone and in seclusion to be at one with the Unborn. One's entire attention is to enter into unionship with the Unborn Spirit. The great wordless and imageless transfer of self-identity.

2. Be of Humble Heart

DISCOURSE TWO

A counsel to embrace a Humble Spirit,
And to the Nature of this Work.

Wake-up, weak creature, and be aware of
what you pretend to be. Do you find yourself
as being somehow special to be called to
partake in this holy favor of the Blessed One?
In truth you are filled with a slothful-spirit
and thus fail to see the auspicious nature of
the work set before you. In this most delicate
time when you find yourself to be most
vulnerable, beware of the dark whisperings of
Mara and his minions as they attempt to
distract and turn you away from this holy
path. Never be deceived by the evil one into
thinking that you can just rest on your past
laurels. To the contrary, you are now being
called to see what you really are, a sorry sack
of bones laden with skandhic sheaths. You
will be forever lost unless you turn-about and
properly discern the nature of this higher-
calling. Far from remaining self-conceited you
ought to be more humble of heart and mind
and thus awaken to the True Nature that is
yours in Spirit alone. Recollect that out of a
legion of fellow-adepts the Unborn Lord has

called you forth to be of singular regard for himself alone. He will lead you to countless Buddhafields that shine majestically in Infinite Light. Then you will be instilled with the Beatific wonder that is the Nirvanic Kingdom of Self. So go forth now and never look back upon your samsaric-past that will only hinder you in your divine quest. It doesn't matter now what you have formally achieved; instead be mindful of what you are still lacking, for that is the best way to be instilled with a spirit of humility. You are to be exclusively about one thing only—to advance further along the path of perfection and thus see the Real Face that was yours before you were born. Beware, though, the Unborn Lord will not tolerate others meddling in your spiritual affairs. You are to be Alone now with Him and no-one else. That is why it is forever necessary to guard the windows of your soul unless the foul vermin that lurk about succeeds in devouring you. If you faithfully abide in these admonitions all you need do is to incessantly court the Lord's pleasure; it will be his breath alone that fills your days and nights in abundant solitude. Proceed forward then, and let us see how you fare.

Commentary

Slothful-spirit: in monastic-circles this is usually referred to as falling victim to a dark spirit of *acedia*. This is a most dangerous occurrence wherein the spirit of the evil one can suck you dry with a horrible unending torpor that weakens your spiritual vitality, thus preventing you from developing further on your path. Make no mistake about it, this is a crucial discourse to constantly be mindful of; it's always in the early stages of wanting to spiritually advance that the dark powers of the evil one will be felt most vividly in this time of vulnerability. One must be forever vigilant and Recollect that now is the time to defeat them less they devour you whole in body, mind, and spirit. Remember, if you think that your past merits alone will protect and advance you further along this way you are sadly mistaken. Cultivating a spirit of humility is key to inviting higher spiritual agencies to come to your aid and empower you to defeat evil and thus claim your rightful spiritual inheritance.

3. Contemplation: The Best Work

DISCOURSE THREE

How to proceed in Contemplation;
Verily, the best work above all others.

Lift up your heart and mind to the Blessed
One, stirring within your depths naught but
Him alone. Focus exclusively on IT and nothing else—this is to be your sole concern. Be
no longer troubled about the created things of
the world, whether human, animal, or lowly
flora. This includes all your former loves and
relationships. Just let them be and take no
further thought or concern about them. This
is known as the Contemplative work of the
Spirit that pleases the Unborn Lord above all
else. All the Buddhas and Bodhisattvas and
Dharma Protectors take great joy in this
endeavor and hasten to assist you in your
determined efforts. Mara and his evil minions
are enraged when you engage in this work,
and will stop at nothing to forestall and
destroy it. Even though you may not
understand how, but all the sentient beings
and worlds are marvelously enriched by your
labors. Even the wretched souls in Avīci Hell
are deeply touched and their agonies soothed
by the effects of this contemplative work; in

16

turn, you too are purified and made whole. Let it be made known that this is the sweetest of all exercises, most pleasing to the Blessed One above all others; yet most difficult to accomplish in itself and by yourself without the aid of divine agencies. Stop wavering but proceed unhindered with great joy as your servant. In the beginning, you will experience only a lingering sense of nothingness hovering about your mind—a cloud of unknowing. Try as you might to overcome this, know that it is good and an invitation to be drawn ever more closely to your Unborn Lord. IT will abide undeterred betwixt you and the Divine Absolute. Above all, never fear IT but instead learn to be at home within IT. Return to IT again and again. It's the closest way you can experience the Blessed One in this lifetime. So then, trust in IT wholeheartedly and you will soon come to that place that is reserved for you alone.

Commentary

Early intimations within The Cloud that speak of the gentle stirrings of Divine Love that is experienced only in the Contemplative-Way. Once engaged in wholeheartedly, you will no longer feel the need for creature comforts but only solace in IT alone.

IT: this form of address will be found throughout the work and refers to the Unborn Lord, as well as that Cloud of Unknowing that works in ways of gentle darkness within your spirit. It refers to That which is Unborn, Uncomposed, Undying, and Uncreated. The original author knew intuitively that this form of contemplative work alone offers great comfort, not only to the adept who is engaged in IT, but through IT by extending Divine Grace to all others as well. The Work Alone can and does achieve this. It's a two-way vehicle, both the one engaged in IT and others somehow mysteriously receive this form of grace.

Cloud of Unknowing: first reference to The Cloud within the work. As stated above, never fight against IT but welcome IT unequivocally. It's only in this fashion, by returning to IT again and again that the doors of the unknowable and unnamable will be opened. IT alone will introduce the way of the via negativa that is the best course of sharing in that divine intimacy.

4. The Littleness of Creation

DISCOURSE FOUR

On the simplicity of Contemplation;
It can neither be acquired through
The intellect nor by imagination.

In order that you do not err in this endeavor, or misconstrue IT as something IT is not, I shall relay something of its true nature to the best of my ability. Contemplation does not require a great amount of time; in fact, it is the shortest work that one can imagine. It's as brief as a split-second, something that is considered by philosophers as the smallest particle of time itself. Because of its littleness it is barely perceivable. Concerning this understanding it is written that, "Of all the time given to you, you will be asked how you spent quality time with the Unborn Lord." Beware, you will be held accountable for how you undertake given those quality moments of your lifespan. To be human is the greatest gift possible, for you will not be given such an opportunity again in millions of lifetimes. It is a matter of the working power of your soul, namely your will. It is for this reason that whoever is reshaped by the ordinances of one's rightly observed will that one can taste nirvana itself in this very life. Do you comprehend now why you have been called to this work? You were made for contemplation, and all of creation rejoices in your noble efforts to realize it completely. When contemplation is not adhered to, then one becomes alien to the beauty of their own Self-nature. Adhering to IT, one enters into communion with the Tathagatas themselves. Hence, be attentive to time and use it wisely. Yet, you hesitate saying, "How can I possibly accomplish this? I'm older now but no wiser. I have seldom paid attention to what has occurred in the past; in fact, how can I possibly make amends now, when instead, my past actions have already reinforced the curse of karma upon my spirit. I am eternally doomed to repeat what was unwisely spent. Please help me for the sake of the Blessed One." It is most wise that you say "for the sake of the Blessed One," for it is in his spirit that you shall find liberation. It has indeed been the power over time and timeless deeds. By remaining faithful you will enter into fellowship with all the Buddhas and Bodhisattvas in all ten directions. Their friends shall be your companions; by companions I mean Arya Tara, Who is the very Primordial Mother of the Buddhas themselves; through her grace you will find strength and the ability to walk hand in hand with all the Bodhisattvas like the Compassionate Avalokiteśvara and the Noble Mañjuśrī who will fill you with holy prajñā (wisdom). Therefore, pay close attention and devoutly discern and undividedly attend to the work of Contemplation and the marvelous ways IT will interact with your own spirit and mind. If it is to be genuine IT will suddenly come upon you like a Divine Spark descending from the heavens. It will be wonderful to behold just how many of these divine stirrings will occur in just one measure of time to the one who is faithfully beholden to this work. Let no-thing persuade you otherwise. If by chance some created care should suddenly assail you in your task, fear not because in your resolute determination you will be empowered to disregard it and return to your holy work. Now we must attend to the difference between Contemplation and the counterfeits that mar your advancement, daydreaming, fantasies, or other false imaginations. Many of these occurrences occur due to an insipid spirit, but moreover they can be induced by Mara the evil one; the outcome is always the same, untamed arrogance at the expense of diligent study and Right Contemplation that is born of a temperate spirit. Indeed, if not tempered in such manner, then the adept places oneself in serious spiritual jeopardy. So for the love of the Blessed One, take prudent care in your spiritual exercises, thus never allowing a false imagination to run amok and hence ruin your hard won cultivation. By all means, never become confused. When I refer to "darkness" or a "cloud", I'm not implying to some form of phenomena that will cloud your mind, but rather an "absence of knowing." Whatever you may have formally known is now alien and dark to you, because you can no longer envision them through spiritual eyes. Hence, It is known as a "Cloud of Unknowing", one that is betwixt you and the Unborn Lord.

Commentary

I'm older now. In the original text it is 24 years of age, something that I discussed in an earlier blog about how I was the same age when I was first introduced to The Cloud. Here, I wanted to make it all inclusive for the benefit of our readership.

Arya Tara: In Unborn Mind Zen she is the equivalent of the Virgin Mary.

Imagination run amok: this same caveat is issued in the Lankavatara Sutra, wherein imagination gives birth to a confused state of mind.

Spiritual eyes: now seeing with the eyes of the Buddhas, or the eye of transcendent wisdom. As such, it is only concerned with the higher realities of the Tathagatas and can no longer worry or be involved with the affairs of the lower bhumis; in time they even stop being aware of them. This is in no way being callous concerning the lower affairs, it is just the Reality of the Dharmadhatu, samsara just dissolves away.

5. The Cloud of Forgetting

DISCOURSE FIVE

*During Contemplation all creatures great and small
Past, present and future
And all the works of those self-same creatures
Must be hidden in a Cloud of Forgetfulness*

If you proceed to enter into this cloud as I have instructed you, keep foremost in mind that there is one more thing you need to do. Just as the Cloud of Unknowing is above betwixt you and the Unborn Lord, so should you also put a Cloud of Forgetting beneath you and all created things. You may imagine that you are somehow far and away from the Blessed One because of this Cloud of Unknowing. But in reality you are from IT if you do not place a Cloud of Forgetting beneath you and all creatures that are constantly vying for your attention. When I refer to all creatures, I am not merely referring to them alone but also to the myriad things they are associated with. Here I make no exception. You must never associate yourself with any creature, either material or spiritual and whether they be good or evil. Let there be no misunderstanding: you are to put all of them and their deeds out of your mind permanently, beneath that Cloud of Forgetting. Even though in the past these associations have brought you some good merit, in this Contemplative Work they are a total hindrance. Remembrance can be a wonderful thing since the eyes of the spirit attempt to bring a ray of spiritual understanding to all undertakings; but if this spiritual faculty continues to be focused on things below then it shall have no room for your charge of being Undividedly One with the Unborn Lord. A cluttered mind leaves no room for the Unborn. At the same time, it will do you no good to focus on those Holy things above, such as the Bodhisattvas and all their marvelous works; or Blessed Arya Tara or Avalokiteśvara in their works of compassion; or the myriad spiritual beings such as the devas who inspire you ever onwards in spiritual awareness and growth; or even the joys of Nirvana. Even though you believe that they are necessary in your spiritual formation, they too will prove to be an obstacle in your Unborn Union. This also extends to the inestimable attributes of the Blessed One Himself; it is far better that you simply rest in naked attentiveness as he is in Itself alone.

Commentary

Cloud of Forgetting: I can remember that even as a young man I suffered from an endless array of forgetfulness. Looking back on it now I can see that it was a good thing, since it allowed me the good fortune of focusing and contemplating on the holy things of spiritual nature. This chapter is short but of crucial value and insight, for the Contemplative Way does not involve the use of intellection in thinking about the Unborn, or about its identification through use of its faculty of action. Meister Eckhart himself stated that one needs to "forget about God". To enter into the Cloud of Unknowing is to rise above even Mind itself, and the Cloud of Forgetting blinds mind's awareness faculty from anything that is not of the Unborn. Both clouds are necessary. John of the Cross referred to the Cloud of Forgetting as the Dark Night of the Senses.

Past Associations: It's a good thing to recollect all those beautiful people and things that brought you great joy in your past, but as stated they will be nothing more than a direct and ongoing hindrance to spiritual growth in the Unborn. You are called to make a choice:

either for past associations, or for total and unequivocal Union with the Unborn, minus all the chatter. This even concerns all those good spiritual associations you once had and hold to be very dear, in essence, they are as nothing compared to what will be "even beyond experience" itself in Divine Unionship. Once that union occurs, all former angst will be eradicated.

6. Light

DISCOURSE SIX

How to abstain from thoughts in Contemplation
Especially those arising from curiosity or natural wit.

If any thought should intrude attempting to
obscure that cloud above you, asking
incessantly "what is it you seek?" To any of
them simply reply, "It is the Unborn Alone
that I seek." Then if they should inquire,
"Who is this Unborn?" respond by saying
"Nothing conceivable or perceivable." Simply
say to them all, "You are powerless to grasp
IT, keep still." Yet left unruffled they will
continue to ask you, "What is it like, what are
the wonderful things it reveals to you?" They
will even impose thoughts of what it was like
long ago when you were young and carefree,
oblivious to such high spiritual ambitions.
Also, they will inflict those sinful conditions
that you once fell victim to and have left an
indelible imprint on your life. Soon enough,
listening to all of them will soon have you
confused and dazed and diverting your
attention from the rightful spiritual work at
hand. Yet, you may find yourself asking,
"These thoughts weren't all that bad, they
have much truth in them." Nevertheless, it is

vitally necessary that you must totally abandon such intimations and place them far beneath that cloud of forgetting. If this is not faithfully carried out, then you shall never come to one day pierce that cloud of unknowing betwixt you and the Unborn. Hence, whenever you are drawn to Contemplation, lift-up your mind and heart with a gentle stirring of Recollection of being as One with your Unborn Lord. You will also find it helpful to choose one word that will center and keep you focused on your one necessary mission of Light. In fact, a word like Light will do most nicely, as long as it has just one-syllable. Then, affix it within the mind so that no-thing can dislodge it. This word will be your strength and your shield against Mara and his evil ones. With this one word you shall subdue all unnecessary mind chatter and consign it beneath that cloud of forgetting. And should one annoying thought come along and distract you, just gently repeat this word over and over. If ever the thought should occur of trying to intellectually analyze this one word, say back that you alone have IT whole and undivided. If you continue in this vein those lingering vexations will no longer assail you. Why? Because you will no longer allow them to feed on those sweet meditations of the Unborn we touched on before.

Commentary

Nothing conceivable or perceivable: a favorite quote from Nisargadatta Maharaj.

One word: This word is known as a spiritual watchword. In time it can even become a form of mantra that serves as a cancellation of all forms of mind distractions.

Light: a word often associated with spiritual enlightenment. For a Lankavatarian this takes on special significance, when Pure Luminous Mind has been Self-Realized and is now a fully enlightened Tathatic-Spirit—occurring in the Bardo of Dharmata.

7. Good or Evil

DISCOURSE SEVEN

Why certain doubts may arise in this work
The necessity of quelling one's own curiosity and reason
Distinguishing the various degrees between the active
And Contemplative life

Now you are asking me: "What is the nature
of these thoughts that press me onward in this
Contemplative work. Are they Good or Evil?
If they are indeed evil, then why do they
arouse so much devotion within my spirit?
There are times that they even bring me great
comfort amidst the misery of this life. With
good reason I believe that these thoughts
continue to bring good fortune as well. So, if
it is indeed true that they are not evil but only
good, then why would you still insist that I
place them beneath the cloud of forgetting?"
Your questions are very good and I will try
my best to address them. Firstly, when you
ask me what is the nature of these thoughts
that remain most persistent, apparently
bringing you good fortune? They are sharp
persuasions that are created in your natural
intellect and bracketed with reason. Secondly,
you ask whether they are good or evil, I will
say that in themselves they are mostly good

because they originate out of your own natural intelligence; this is a reflection of Divine input because IT will not contradict Itself even within the human construct. However, be aware that you are inclined to use them for both good and evil. It is good when they are illumined with Unborn Light, in this sense I'm not surprised that they bring you times of good fortune. But beware that they can as easily become evil when they are swollen with pride, rabid mental curiosity, and when the ego becomes enamored of itself out of exclusive study and appliance of spiritual principles. This is the stuff of haughtiness in the minds of conceited scholars wherein they can become masters of deceit and vanity and falsehood. This is a warning that is also meant for everyone, especially those engaged in material affairs in the desire-realm of Kamadhatu. Next, you inquire why you should place such thoughts beneath the cloud of forgetting when they are of good benefit. In order to best address this it needs to be made known that there are two walks of life: the active and the Contemplative. The active life is the lower while the Contemplative is the higher. Within the active life there are two degrees, a lower and a higher, and within the

Contemplative life there are also two degrees, a lower and a higher. Both of them are inseparably complementary even though they remain distinct in themselves. Why? Because the highest part of the active life is the same as the lower part of the contemplative. This being the case one is not wholly active unless some aspect of the Contemplative is present, likewise for those who participate in the Contemplative—some aspect of the active remains. The active part begins and ends in samsara, but is not the case with the Contemplative. Within scripture, Mary has chosen the best part that can never be taken away. The active life is always filled with much anxiety and tension, while the Contemplative Life rests in the Unborn alone. The lower-part of the active life consists in corporal works of mercy. The higher part of the active life and the lower part of the contemplative consists in observing times of meditation—the time when one begins to focus on the things of the spirit that can assist one in attaining good merits. While the higher part of Contemplation is exclusively concerned in partaking in the spiritual darkness of the cloud of unknowing, becoming immersed in the Unborn Alone. Again, the lower-part is directed outwardly, mostly with an extrovert posture beneath oneself thereby being concerned with the things below. The higher-part (lower stage of contemplation) is more interiorly directed, wherein you begin to discern spiritual reality. But in the direct higher-part of Contemplation, all of your concern and effort is directed exclusively between you and the Unborn. This is all about transcending yourself and now depending on higher spiritual agencies to point towards what you cannot do with those lower energies', direct Union with the Absolute Lordship. Furthermore, one begins to discern that it is impossible for the adept to approach the higher part of the active life unless he learns to abandon the lower part. Similarly, it's impossible to approach the higher part of Contemplation unless one weans oneself away from the lower. It would also be wrong for an adept who is engaged in meditation, indeed a direct hindrance, for him to be turning his attention to his good and charitable works regardless of how meaningful and worthwhile they were. Likewise, it would be detrimental for one who is engaged in the darkness of the cloud of unknowing to be thinking about how wonderful and compassionate the works of the Blessed One are—since they would prove to be a direct distraction from one's attentiveness to the Unborn ITself. Forget and erase from your mind how much comfort these images can be. They have absolutely no place in this imageless work. So let-go of these very clever and persuasive thoughts. Place all of them beneath that cloud of forgetting, no matter how beneficial and holy they appear in your mindset. Recollect that forever how long your spirit inhabits this mortal carcass, your thought patterns are useless in decoding the nature of the Unborn Absolute. Thinking in any way less will surely lead you into grave error.

Commentary

But beware that they can as easily become evil: one must keep careful watch of what originates in the intellect, no matter how pure the thoughts may appear to be, because underneath they can be hiding some ulterior motive, such is the habit of pride and its swollen ego. This oftentimes occurs in those who feign to possess some great and heretofore unknown knowledge. Their bogus imprints always leaves nasty marks and thus unmasks their true ignorance of such matters.

Active vs. Contemplative: in spiritual circles the active life is always considered to be lower than the majestic workings that offers itself in the Contemplative lifestyle. But the author also takes great pains here to relay how they both intersect each other. There are elements of the higher in the lower, such as when the corporal work of charity begins to cultivate great merit and compassion. And then there are elements of the lower in the higher, when the stages of deep meditation begin to give birth to higher states of awareness. Traditionally the corporal works of charity are as follows:

To feed the hungry. To give water to the thirsty. To clothe the naked. To shelter the homeless. To visit the sick. To visit the imprisoned, or ransom the captive. To bury the dead.

Mary has chosen the best part: again, a scriptural reference (Luke 10:38-42) concerning Mary and Martha. Mary has chosen the Contemplative and hence best part; Martha is always busy about mundane affairs and hence has chosen the lower part.

It would be detrimental for one who is engaged in the darkness of the cloud of unknowing to be thinking about how wonderful and compassionate the works of

the Blessed One are: here we see where the
author's true allegiance lies, with the higher
Contemplative element. All of this business of
higher vs. lower was a custom of the time
(and remains so to this very day) since many
people were actively involved in ministry in
some form or other. It's usually only after
coming into contact with the needs of others
that the Spirit of Compassion is understood in
a broader sense encompassing prayer,
community, and service. It is afterwards when
the Great Contemplative Calling presents
Itself when one is drawn to the Absolute
Source of that compassion.

8. Taste it

DISCOURSE EIGHT

How even the most holiest thoughts
Induce a direct hindrance
To the work of Contemplation.

Recollect then, that when you attend to your
Contemplative Spirit, all manner of
conceptualizations must be subdued before
they subdue you. In regard to this, you will
find when you perceive yourself to be in the
depths of the Dark Contemplation that is the
direct moment that these thought forms — as
well hidden as they be— always lie in wait to
assail your spirit. Hence, learn to eradicate
such images no matter how inviting they may
appear to be before your mind's eye. For I tell
you this: in order for your spirit to remain
healthy it needs to perpetually have a taste of
the Divine before it always. This taste is more
pleasing to the Unborn Lord and all Buddha's
and Bodhisattvas, yea even your family and
friends, than anything else you may attempt to
do. It is a requirement for your better health
of mind and spirit as well as a spiritual benefit
for your loved ones. Such is the secret
pressing of this cloud of unknowing that
outshines the brilliance of any Deva or other

spiritual being that brings great bliss. None of this should surprise you. Once you grasp the truth of my words you will come to a better understanding. Taste IT, and IT will be with you always. Rest assured, no one shall ever have a clearer insight than this succulent taste of the Unborn. Hence, lift up your heart and soul to this loving cloud, or better still, allow the Blessed One to draw you up into this cloud. I promise you, you will soon put to rest all other things. Again, Recollect; if the smallest thought form should overcome and subdue you, how much more will you be obstructed if you willingly cultivate such rubbish during the blessed work of Contemplation? And if the presence of any pure spiritual agency hinders your progress, then how much more the remembrance of any created being in this life will definitely obstruct you in your Contemplative work? Please keep in mind that I'm not saying that these thoughts, particularly of any higher spiritual agency in the Unborn are malignant in themselves; heaven forbid if you should misunderstand me. What I am stressing is that they can be more of a hindrance than a help. If you are seeking IT above all else, then you will never find gratification with anything less than IT.

Commentary

A taste of the Divine: Our series on The Vajrasamādhi Sutra best sums up what the quality of this single taste is like. It is there that Wǒnhyo states that "Although this person's body appears to be that of an ordinary householder, his mind abides in the single taste, for this single taste absorbs all tastes." There are innumerable Dharmas serving as expedient means to liberate the various sentitalia; yet in all of them there is One Sole Essence, a single-taste, which is the exclusive elixir that quenches their insatiable thirst for deliverance from dukkha.

Loving cloud: this is the core message of the entire text of The Cloud of Unknowing; this form of "love" is not the sort of sentimental rubbish that litters our culture. It is known as *Agape*, or burning with Transcendent Love for the Divine Alone.

9. Spiritual Madness

DISCOURSE NINE

How confused adepts misunderstand the word "in", and the delusions which follow.

The madness of which I'm referring to unfolds like this: they have read and heard it said that they should shut down their exterior senses and strain to turn inwardly. However they misinterpret what "turning-inwardly" means. By turning their external senses inwardly upon themselves they generate untold damage. What they are doing goes directly against the natural order. They imagine that utilizing this "brute-force" technique that they can somehow induce their faculties of seeing and hearing to invite things from the spiritual world. Quite the opposite occurs. They turn themselves into creatures of darkness and in so doing invite evil spirits to enter into their soul and make their evil home therein. Once implanted in the domain of their spirit, Mara and his minions feign all manner of fake sensual pleasures, such as overpowering sweet odors and delectable tastes. And much far worse: creating bizarre impressions in their sexual organs that are accompanied with burning sensations in all the entrails of the body like the lower bowels and other associated organs. These foolish adepts also become confused over the word "up". When hearing such admonitions such as "lifting up one's heart and mind to the Unborn Lord", they stare upwards starry eyed into the heavens in the vain hope of encountering angelic agencies. Other times they hope to encounter some form of extraterrestrial beings who have privy information into the nature of spiritual realities. In so doing they are creating gods in their own image. All in all, this is nothing other than pseudo contemplation at its worst. Yet, they somehow imagine that all of this is the work of the Blessed One, thus forever consigning themselves over to the company of demons. You have been forewarned, all such behavior will lead to irreversible possession. Truth be told, the Real Stuff of the Contemplative Way of the Unborn has no in or out, up or down, right, left, front or back. It is unlimited and undivided and imageless beyond all physical dimensions; for it is never the work of the flesh but a spiritual élan that is the adventure reserved only for the pure of heart.

Commentary

This portrays the pitfalls that can oftentimes
befall one who is engaged in any form of
apparent "spiritual work". Turning inward is a
phrase oftentimes heard in spiritual circles but
is also misrepresented. It's not about a
"physical" turning in; this misunderstanding is
common and can lead to the ruin of a fine
adept whose intentions are good but lacks the
proper and informed direction that can lead
them into the Right Way of Contemplation.
Contemplation, if it's worth its salt, becomes
the very act which the adept becomes attuned
with the inward work of the Unborn Spirit;
and this "inward" work is only done by that
spirit alone and no outside agencies, not even
the mind and soul of the adepts themselves.
Pseudo-contemplation is the work of the evil
one and will always rely upon the adept's
"senses" in gaining entrance and wreaking
untold havoc. If one becomes "giddy" in their
spiritual work then they're not about that
"Real Stuff of the Contemplative Way of the
Unborn". It's a form of spiritual madness and
will only lead to self-destruction. Haughtiness
is another sign of spiritual madness, false
pride. Whatever form of imperfection occurs
should be caught and thoroughly dealt with

before reengaging in any spiritual work. You see, that's why the Lankavatarian adage of "imagelessness" becomes paramount. When rightly employed it will unmask any demon of the senses, those evil "images" (any form, sensation, thought, volition, mortal consciousness). The Cloud of Unknowing is an imageless affair and entering IT will always bring great spiritual blessings and protection untold.

10. The Occupied Mind

DISCOURSE TEN

Unless one understands the power of the mind
One can easily be deceived in the workings of the
Contemplative Spirit;
And how one is transformed through the grace of the
Unborn

Dear Spiritual Friend in the Unborn,
hopefully you are aware of the misery created
because of your brokenness. It is no wonder
then how easily you can become deceived
concerning the True Nature of
Contemplation, particularly due to the
ignorance of the powers of the spirit and the
way in which these powers unfold. Whenever
you find your mind being occupied with
material matters, however some may prove to
be beneficial, recollect that anything of the
physical world is in truth beneath the dignity
of your spirit. And also discern that when
your mind is fully imbibed with the
mysterious workings of your spiritual
faculties, you grow ever-stronger in self-
gnosis. This self-gnosis empowers you to
Right Virtue and in so doing benefits others
along the road to spiritual perfection. But
there will come opportunities when your mind

and spirit are free from any involvement with anything of a material or spiritual nature, thus freeing you to being engaged with the very Essence of the Unborn Absolute. This, then, is the work of Right Contemplation of which I have been describing throughout this work. In this sense you will come to transcend yourself, becoming most Unborn-like, because you have grown in the ways of grace and thus are no longer disturbed by the lowly nature of the material. Yet, you are still not equal to the Unborn As it is in Itself, for IT has no beginning or end and is hence deathless in nature. Thus, my dear spiritual friend, please discern clearly and wisely what I am teaching you. If you remain in ignorance concerning the inner workings of your spiritual faculties, you will be continually deceived in comprehending words that are written exclusively with the ways of the spirit in mind. All of this I must insist lest you try to materially misconstrue with what is intended to be meant spiritually.

Commentary

We have arrived at what is known as a midpoint in an understanding between material and spiritual realities. Of course, we need to co-exist with both since essentially we live in a material world whilst simultaneously attempting to live in a higher spiritual one. But right there is the crux of the problem. The damned bifurcation, or duality of the equation. The Lanka teaches that the material one is a mere fancy of our imagination; and yet, if we depend on material means to enter into those higher spiritual realms, we will be sorely disappointed because through those means we are only recreating samsara on a higher plane. Remember that Mara has his own higher light heavens which can transfix and bewitch one into thinking that they have accessed transcendent Buddha-fields. One can also get lost in astral planes of one's own making. The astral body is like an invisible twin who lives within the recesses of one's spirit and manifests itself oftentimes through dreams and quite frequently through what many refer to on the material plane as a near-death experience. All sorts of trouble and dangers are encountered in those astral planes. It can become confusing when we hear and use the term spiritual, because it can connote all manner of phenomena. Best rule of thumb is to equate spiritual as what occurs within the cloud of unknowing, and that is the [total] absence [negation] of all phenomena; whilst all psycho-physical manifestations should always be placed beneath that cloud of forgetting. Hence, Mind un-occupied.

11. Nowhere Man

DISCOURSE ELEVEN

What is nowhere to the body consciousness is everywhere spiritually;
Our outer-nature ridicules Contemplation as a waste of time

On the same topic, someone may tell you to gather all your strength and worship the Unborn internally. That is all well and good but I don't recommend this since someone may take the advice literally. Always see to it that you are no way "within yourself", nor above, nor below, nor on one side, nor on the other. "Well then," you will ask, "in this line of reasoning I will end-up being nowhere!" That is simply wonderful, for that is where I would have you be, nowhere!" Why? *Because nowhere materially is everywhere spiritually.* Always make sure and be aware that your Contemplative work is completely divorced from the material. Your spiritual work is never in any particular physical place. Recollect that whatever your mind is focusing on, truly you will be there in spirit just as your bodily form is in the location you are physically. Of course, during the course of your Contemplative work, the skandhic mind with

49

its five functions will assume that you are doing nothing because it has nothing to feed upon, nothing to drain your energies away from your spiritual faculties. Never allow those miserable skandhic bandits to gain the upper hand, just continue to persevere in that nothingness with the assurance that the Unborn Lord is always very near at hand. For I tell you truly that it is far better for you to be nowhere bodily, wrestling with your body consciousness, than to reign supreme in the land as some lord of leisure enjoying everything as if you personally owned all of it. I say unto you, abandon the world's "everywhere" and "something" for that marvelous "nothingness" and "nowhere". Don't ever feel anxious that your body consciousness is unable to comprehend IT. All is simply unfolding as it should, for this nothingness is so lofty that nothing in the created order could ever reach IT. For IT can never be understood, dissected, and studied; It can only be lived. For the newly initiated, IT will only appear to be very dark and inscrutable. At this early junction one is blinded by the very splendor of its spiritual light and not by rays of ordinary darkness nor the absence of physical light. So, then, who is this that labels this spiritual wonder as mere emptiness? Only the superficial self and not the Real Self. For the Real Self proclaims IT as the all; but at the same time, as no-thing. For in this Luminous Darkness one intuitively knows the essence of all things, both material and spiritual, devoid of any particular focus to any one thing by itself.

Commentary

This is my favorite discourse since it directly addresses the via negativa of Dionysius. Nowhere constitutes location-less when assigned to materiality; yet it becomes everywhere when assigned to the spirit: the Unborn is everywhere at once and yet nowhere in particular. And it is through the Dark Principle of Nowhere-ness, in the stateless state, that adepts need to find imageless habitation. The Unborn as well is never to be consigned with anything imaginable or intelligible; in this sense IT is always a no-thing.

For the Real Self proclaims IT as the all: John of the Cross Wrote, "In order to be the All, desire to be nothing."

12. Transformation in the Nothingness

DISCOURSE TWELVE

How one's affections are marvelously transformed
In the spiritual experience of the Nothing
Which occurs nowhere

One's whole disposition is wonderfully
transfigured in the spiritual experience of the
nothingness. Yet when the first time one
experiences IT all of one's past transgressions
are paraded before him. Nothing is spared, all
of one's thoughts, emotions and past evil
offences, whether physically or spiritually,
appears before his mind's eye in all their
abject horror. Which anyway one turns they
cling to him like blackened sticky pitch until
they are washed away in tears of agony. There
are times when these excruciating visions
occur that one imagines that he is having
glimpses into the darkest cavities of hell.
Reliving one's past transgressions is so
terrifying that one despairs of never being
freed from them. There are many who have
come thus far in their spiritual journey that
one is tempted to give it all up and return to
the temporary comfort that the physical realm
offers them. In so doing they forsake the
spiritual consolations that would have been

showered upon them had they endured in these trials. One who patiently abides in this darkness will eventually regain confidence in his spiritual destiny. The horrors will continue but there is the fervent trust that they will subside after ongoing these necessary purgation's. They will soon witness their past transgressions washed clean by the gentle and healing touch of the Unborn Lord. Sometimes it seems as if this nothingness is nothing other than some sweet heaven. Ultimately they will arrive at that junction wherein one's gentle repose in this darkness is nothing other than the Unborn itself. Yes! Whatever comes to pass you shall arrive at the self-realization that it is the cloud of unknowing betwixt you and the Unborn.

Commentary

This all bespeaks the necessary ongoing purgation's that must be endured before final transfiguration in the Unborn occurs. All of one's past karma needs to be burned off until one's spirit is tempered with the soothing Luminous Darkness of the Unborn Mind.

13. Sans Senses

DISCOURSE THIRTEEN

The silencing of the skandhas leads to the fruitful
experience of spiritual things;
Likewise in silencing the spiritual faculties we come to
experience the gnosis
Of the Unborn

Continue to work diligently in this
nothingness which is nowhere, and abandon
the use of all your bodily senses; for I tell you
truly that this Noble Contemplative work
cannot even begin to be fathomed through
skandhic lens. Your eyes can only envision
material things by their appearance: its mass,
form, color, and location. Your ears only
function through the vibration of various
sound waves. Your nose is designed to detect
either pleasant or bad odors through olfactory
lobes. Your sense of taste detects sourness or
sweetness, what is salty and fresh, or what is
bitter and unpleasant. And your sense of
touch as to whether something is hot or cold,
hard or soft, smooth or sharp. But the
Unborn knows nothing of these dimensions;
anything spiritual has none of these skandhic
characteristics. Hence, stop attempting to
work here with your bodily senses in any way,

shape, or manner. For all those who attempt to be a contemplative and assume that they can see, hear, smell, taste, or feel their way through this work either interiorly or exteriorly, are working against the natural order. Nature has designed the use of the senses for sensate matter only, never to be used for the direct and intuitive gnosis of spiritual reality. However one can learn much from their failures in attempting to do so. One comes to intuit and hence know more about the ways of the spirit by what they are not, than by what they are. A good proof of this is when hearing or reading about something that our skandhic mind cannot fully decipher, you can rest assured that this subject matter is of the pure spiritual realm and utterly divorced from the material. It needs to equally be stated that our spiritual faculties are also limited in relation to the Unborn As It Is In Itself. Even if someone is well versed in the sutras and the knowledge pertaining to spiritual realities, one will never have enough understanding when it comes to the uncreated and deathless Unborn Lord. Yet, there is a negative-understanding which does have an insight into the Absolute Nature of the Deathless One, the way of the via negativa. It was for this specific reason that St. Dionysius had the best insight, the most supernal gnosis of the Unborn which is only known by non-knowing. Truly anyone who reads the works of St. Dionysius will clearly come to see that everything I've been teaching here, from beginning to end, can be verified through the saints own teaching. Yet, I do not wish to quote him any further or any other spiritual master for that matter. There was, and in some quarters still is, a ruling that no one should speak of any spiritual realities unless it is accompanied with references from scripture or scholarly commentaries; yet, this was, and still is a vain intellectual conceit. I will have none of that here since you really don't have any need for it anyway. Perhaps for a further refinement and spiritual cultivation of what you have experienced in the Unborn, such methods may still be employed at some junction. But in the final analysis, whoever has spiritual ears to hear what I say, let those who are moved to believe, simply believe what they will come to experience in the Unborn. Authentically, there is no other way.

Commentary

Truly the skandhic apparatus (form, sensation, thought, volition, mortal consciousness) is inadequate to learn the ways of the spirit. But even the application of our spiritual faculties can also fail when we encounter a spiritual reality that cannot be adequately conveyed by mind, reason, or will, and then we can rest assured that it must be the incomprehensible Unborn Mind.

Spiritual faculties: faith or conviction or belief (*saddhā*) energy or persistence or perseverance (*viriya*) mindfulness or memory (*sati*) stillness of the mind (*samādhi*) wisdom or understanding or comprehension *(paññā)*.

St. Dionysius: Dionysius the Areopagite. The first and only explicit reference to Pseudo-Dionysius himself, although the entire work of the Cloud is based on his theology. Here the author gives him his due credit. But it should also be said that both the author of the Cloud and the works of John of the Cross eclipsed the Dionysian foundations.

14. Moses and the Cloud

DISCOURSE FOURTEEN.

*Some people only experience the perfection of
Contemplation during rapture,
While others can experience it always at a time of
their choosing, during the
Ordinary moments of one's day.*

Some consider the Contemplative endeavor to
be so heavy and awesome that it cannot be
undertaken without heavy toil, and then only
seldom, when one enters into states of
ecstasy. I will respond to these people to the
best of my ability, though my best before the
Unborn will always be a feeble blip. All such
matters depend upon one's spiritual
dispositions in light of the Unborn. Each
adept carries within them particular talents
and abilities. Hence, the spiritual gift of
Contemplation can only be dispensed
according to each one's capacity. It's true that
some will never reach Contemplation without
first engaging in that very lengthy and arduous
spiritual journey, and then only tasting brief
interludes of spiritual ecstasy. On the other
hand, there are others who are so spiritually
refined with a great intuition in the Unborn
that they can always turn to this

Contemplative work whenever they so desire, during the ordinary routine of one's day, whether sitting, walking, standing, or kneeling. They always seem to gain a sure footing in a healthy balance between both their physical and spiritual faculties. Most of the time they can do so with little or no difficulty. For instance, in the example of Moses we find the first and the example of Aaron, the priest of the temple, we find the second. The renowned Ark of the Covenant is a representation of the grace of contemplation, and those whose lives were connected with the Ark itself fully reveals those who were fervently directed in the Contemplative path. This analogy of the Ark and Contemplation is most appropriate since the Ark itself contained all the jewels and relics of the holy temple, just as, in similar fashion, the heart which is focused on the Unborn Lord in the cloud of unknowing contains all the virtues of the spirit which is hidden in the temple of the Unborn. Before Moses could see the ark itself and learn how it was to be constructed, he had to make the steep climb, along with a burdensome effort to reach the mountain's peak. Once upon the plateau he had to remain there and work within the cloud for six days, after which on the seventh day the Lord descended to give him the instructions on how the Ark was to be erected. Hence, Moses's difficult and strenuous labors and his hindered vision symbolize those who cannot reach the full height of this spiritual work without such initial efforts and strenuous toil; even then the full revelation is seldom seen and is totally dependent upon consent of the Unborn Spirit. But what Moses found exhausting and seldom received, Aaron already possessed IT. As a temple priest, Aaron had the power and the permission to enter into the Holy of Holies and contemplate upon the Ark whenever he so desired. Hence, Aaron symbolizes those I described earlier, who by their spiritual acumen and the assistance from divine agencies, can make the perfection of this Contemplative work their own whenever they so desired.

Commentary

This is the actual story from Exodus 24: "Then went up Moses, and Aaron, Nadab, and Abbioud, and seventy of the elders of Israel: And they saw the God of Israel. And upon the nobles of the children of Israel he laid not his hand: also they saw God, and did eat and drink. And the LORD said unto Moses, Come up to me into the mount, and be there: and I will give thee tables of stone, and a law, and commandments which I have written; that thou mayest teach them. And Moses rose up, and his minister Joshua: and Moses went up into the mount of God. And he said unto the elders, Tarry ye here for us, until we come again unto you: and, behold, Aaron and Hur are with you. And Moses went up into the mount, and a cloud covered the mount. And the glory of the LORD abode upon Mount Sinai, and the cloud covered it six days: and the seventh day he called unto Moses out of the midst of the cloud. And the sight of the glory of the LORD was like devouring fire on the top of the mount. And Moses went into the midst of the cloud, and Moses was in the mount forty days and forty nights." The author of the Cloud's metaphorical point is that Moses was the messenger, while Aaron the priest had special privy knowledge of the Ark due to his office. The basic sense of all this is that the Cloud's author found the latter (the effortless way) as being superior. One should not judge between the two. It may take a novice a long while, sometimes even years, to reach Contemplative maturity. But this doesn't make one any less-than the seasoned contemplative. After all, Moses is indeed more renowned in the bible than Aaron, even though Aaron had priestly privileges. The work of Spiritual Cultivation, as Tsung-Mi would agree, is worth its weight in gold over initial sudden awakening.

15. Retrospection

DISCOURSE FIFTEEN

Those inclined toward Contemplation
Will come to recognize that what has been written
In this work is akin to his own spirit;
Thus a reiteration of the prologue is needed

If it appears to you that this Contemplative work is not suited to your own spirituality or temperament, take leave of it and seek out good spiritual consul that will direct you in a way that is best for your spirit. If that is to be the case I ask you to please excuse all I have written here for your spiritual benefit. Before you take leave of it, read it over again two or three times. In that way you may come to better appreciate it and enlighten you more as to its content. All will unfold as it should when you read it again and again. It is my fervent hope that you will do this. Remember, too, don't share this content with anyone else unless you are absolutely sure that they are capable of comprehending its message. For instance, don't discuss this work with anyone who doesn't have a contemplative disposition and temperament. Review the discourse wherein I describe the type of person who can benefit from this Contemplative work. If you should share it with another, always impress upon him the absolute importance of reading it through from beginning to end. If it should come to pass that someone reads only one section and not the rest that complements it, then they will experience utmost mental and spiritual confusion. If there's any part of this work that needs greater clarification, please alert me and I will amend it. All in all, though, I prefer that you never share this work with gossipers, ne'er-do-wells, excessive fault-finders, and all those with mean-dispositions. It is definitely not for any of them, whether they be educated or not. Some may even come to it with the best of intentions, yet they are so caught up exclusively with the active life that this work could not possibly offer anything to them.

Commentary

This discourse is essentially a paraphrase of the opening prologue. The author of the cloud is adamant that this work is not meant for just anyone and even for those who begin the work, may in time come to experience no benefit in it. Authentic Contemplation is no easy endeavor and requires years of painstaking effort and above all, endless patience. Many people come to it because they are intrigued with the subject matter, it all sounds so wonderfully esoteric in nature, but in reality it is all about good plain old-fashioned hard work and forever being spiritually earnest. It's solemn in nature, but the eventual spiritual rewards are worth the time and effort.

16. Spiritual Signs

DISCOURSE SIXTEEN

*Some spiritual signs that show one is being
Called to Contemplation.*

Many who read these words may find them
fascinating and thereafter feel compelled to
take up the work of Contemplation, but are
by no means being called to this spiritual path.
Their inner compulsion may indeed be
indicative of natural or even excessive
curiosity. The following signs will prove
helpful in the ongoing discernment of being
authentically called. Let one first discern if
they've done everything possible to cleanse
their mind for such an endeavor. Firstly, the
practice of the six paramitas accompanied
with good consultation with a competent
spiritual director. As time goes on let one fully
discern that Contemplation is foremost on
their mind, thus attracting their attention
more than ordinary meditation or other
spiritual discipline. Furthermore, if they
discover that nothing they do, whether of a
physical or spiritual nature offers any peace of
mind except this mystical-drawing to the
gentle cloak of the cloud leading them further
into the Unborn, then this is a definite sign

that the Unborn Lord is calling them to such a holy union. If these signs are absent, then I can absolutely assure you that one is not being called. Please be mindful that those being called to Contemplation will not always feel these mystical yearnings right from the beginning, because this is surely not the case. A beginner adept will sense these signs being withdrawn from time to time. Sometimes IT is being withdrawn from him so that he doesn't become prideful and automatically assume that he can control It whenever he likes. In point of fact, whenever the cloud is being withdrawn, more often than not one's own arrogance is the leading cause. Oftentimes the neophyte automatically assumes that this absence means that the Unborn is his enemy, when in truth IT is his best friend. But as usually is the case the apprentice finds IT being withdrawn because of his own carelessness; the result is that one is horribly consumed with pain and remorse. Occasionally, the Unborn Lord does withdraw IT, but only so that IT is more deeply appreciated. The greatest grace occurs when one assumes that he has lost IT, because he then discovers an inner-strength that one-pointedly draws him back to the Unborn work with a fervor he never experienced before. If this be the case, then it is truly an unmistakable sign that the Unborn Lord is calling you to become a Contemplative. Remember, it is not what or who you have been in countless past lives, but what the Unborn would have you be. If you begin to experience less and less joys in past endeavors and former spiritual encounters, then truly know that you are indeed marked out for the Unborn. Farewell, dear spiritual friend, may the Unborn's blessing and mine be upon you! May you come to experience that True Peace and wise counsel that only comes from the Unborn alone. Svaha.

Commentary

The six paramitas:

"Generosity is a practice leading to liberation whereby one gives freely of one's body, possessions and merits. This fulfills the hopes of living beings, dispels avarice, and makes one confident, fearless and honored by all."

"Ethics is a practice leading to liberation whereby the effects of evil actions and the influence of the kleśas are purified. It causes one to become revered among all people, and to gather them together without threats or force. Proper ethics are therefore guarded with the utmost care by the wise."

"Patience is a practice leading to liberation which is the most excellent attribute of powerful persons. It is the most effective ascetic or spiritual practice for those beset by kleśas. It is the best weapon against the great enemy, anger. It is the best defense against harmful words, etc. Because of this, patience must be cultivated and practiced by every possible means available."

"Firm and unremitting effort is a practice leading to liberation which causes the good qualities of learning and understanding to continually increase. Through effort, all activities become meaningful, and whatever work is begun, is then finished in accordance with the goal. Understanding this, Bodhisattvas generate a great force of effort which dispels all indolence."

"Meditation is a practice leading to liberation whereby one gains complete control over one's mind. When settled in meditation, one gains the power of peace and stability. After arising from meditation, all virtuous actions may be readily engaged, and the body and mind take on a blissful sense of fitness and well-being. Understanding this, great yogins continually adhere to the practice of concentration which destroys the great enemy of distraction."

"Wisdom is the faculty which perceives profound Suchness. It is the technique which finally and completely uproots samsara. It is the treasure-trove of virtue and accomplishment universally praised in all of the sacred texts. It is the supreme method for clearing away the darkness of ignorance and delusion. Understanding this, those who truly desire liberation make unceasing efforts to generate wisdom." (ref: Tsongkhapa)

Finding a competent teacher (guru) in whatever spiritual path you choose is not an easy endeavor. It takes trial and effort. You may choose someone in the beginning, only to later discover that he or she is not best suited to your authentic path of who you are called to be in the Unborn. What is most often the case is that one day you may simply outgrow that director, and then it is worth your spiritual cultivation and edification to move on.

Cloud Epilogue

The author of The Cloud knew what he
wanted to convey to his audience but had no
clear systematic plan designed to carry it out.
Without question his writing is most fluid
with a fine contemplative spirit but mostly
writes with whatever is coming into his mind
at the moment. One possible reason being
that he was in daily-session with his young
neophyte and the discussion pertains to the
actual growth of that adept's mind at a given
time frame. But as time progresses one can
ascertain that he's also addressing a wider
audience, although one within the confines of
a monastic setting. This fact is driven home
time and time again that the cloud is not
meant for just anyone along the paths of
spirituality, but one who was being drawn to
this specific and singular way of
contemplation. By and large, the key to
understanding the cloud can be found within
the first three discourses, while the remaining
ones is about driving the message home with
comments and expansion on his themes along
with necessary Contemplative praxsis. One is
reminded here that the neophyte is being
called to an advanced stage in the spiritual life.
And this must be carried out with the utmost

diligence and humility. Along with this is his incessant message that the created order of things must be placed beneath that cloud of forgetting, before the deeper and more lasting work of entering into the transcendent cloud of unknowing can occur. Contemplation is an arduous path and is very hard to live given the fact of one's brokenness. While spiritual consolations come along the way, one experiences mostly dryness and utter emptiness in the hope of that dark void being filled with the Luminous Light of the Divine. Once again this is why the work is bracketed with those admonitions that this way of life is not for those who are merely inquisitive but rather for those whose spirit remains vigilant despite the ongoing spiritual attacks from the evil one. If one perseveres, then the prize of absolute Union with the Divine will occur. As stated in the introduction, this rendition of The Cloud of Unknowing is written especially for a wider audience in mind, particularly of Buddhist sway. Certain spiritual themes are universal in nature and certainly the cloud offers the best of that apophatic mysticism. But mostly the emphasis here is on that work of Contemplation. Contemplation in the Way of the Unborn has been written about in different venues here at Unborn Mind Zen. Hopefully the regular reader will ascertain by now that this form of infused contemplation fits quite nicely in a Buddhist framework. Perhaps even more so, one would be hard pressed to find anything of similar import pertaining to contemplation versus meditation for a Buddhist Mystic anywhere else on the internet. In this sense we take great pride in our mission here of advancing the Contemplative Spirit in Light of the Unborn. May the Light of the Unborn remain with you always,

Vajragoni

*Vajragoni can be reached at:

vajragoni@unbornmind.com

www.ingramcontent.com/pod-product-compliance
Lightning Source LLC
Chambersburg PA
CBHW060144050426
42448CB00010B/2293